The Magic School Bus
on the Ocean Floor

The Magic School Bus
on the Ocean Floor

By Joanna Cole   Illustrated by Bruce Degen

SCHOLASTIC INC. / New York

Library of Congress Cataloging-in-Publication Data

Cole, Joanna.
The magic school bus on the ocean floor / by Joanna Cole;
illustrated by Bruce Degen.
p. cm.
Summary: On another special field trip on the magic school
bus, Ms. Frizzle's class learns about the ocean and the
different creatures that live there.
ISBN 0-590-41430-5
1. Marine fauna — Juvenile literature. 2. Ocean bottom —
Juvenile literature. [1. Ocean. 2. Marine animals.]
I. Degen, Bruce, ill. II. Title.
QL122.2.C65   1992
591.92—dc20   91-17695
CIP
AC

12 11 10 9 8 7 6 5 4 3 2 1   2 3 4 5 6 7/9
Printed in the U.S.A.   36

First Scholastic printing, September 1992

For the paintings in this book, the illustrator used pen and
ink, watercolor, color pencil, and gouache.

The ocean animals and plants are labeled only at their
first appearance within the story.

The author and illustrator wish to thank John D. Buck, Ph.D.,
Professor of Marine Sciences, Marine Science Institute,
The University of Connecticut, for his assistance
in preparing this book.

For their helpful advice and consultation, thanks also to
Dr. Susan Snyder, Program Director, Teacher Preparation
and Enrichment, National Science Foundation; Dr. Michael
Reeve, Division of Ocean Sciences, National Science
Foundation; Cindy Stong, Professor of Marine Biology,
Bowling Green State University; Mr. Maxwell Cohen; and the
staffs at the National Aquarium, Baltimore; the Thames
Science Center, New London, Connecticut; and the American
Museum of Natural History.

To Margo, Bruce, Emily, and Beth, with love
J.C.

For Mom and Dad and summer days at the beach
B.D.

It was the end of the day,
and it was *hot* in school.
We had been working for hours
on our ocean science projects.
All our work made Ms. Frizzle very happy.
But it made *us* very tired and hot.

SWIMMERS IN THE SEA
by Shirley, John and Ralph

FISH - Sweeps tail from side to side

WHALE - Moves tail up and down

JELLYFISH - Opens body like an umbrella, then closes rapidly to jet upward

SQUID - takes in water and forces it out to jet forward or backward

SCALLOP - opens and closes shell rapidly to move.

This is my sculpture of a HUMUHUMUNUKUNUKUAPUAA A FISH THAT LIVES IN HAWAII (THE NAME IS LONGER THAN THE FISH) —ALEX

Chart of uncharted Seas.

We were putting the finishing touches on a display about how ocean animals swim when someone said, "I wish *we* could go swimming."

Ms. Frizzle looked up.
Without warning, she said,
"As a matter of fact, children,
I've been planning a class trip to the ocean
for tomorrow."
Everybody cheered.
Sometimes having a weird teacher isn't so bad!

DID SHE SAY OCEAN?

WHERE WE CAN SWIM AND PLAY?

IS SHE SERIOUS?

DON'T ASK, JUST PACK YOUR BEACH BAG!

WHY IS THE OCEAN SALTY?
by Tim
Much of the salt in the ocean water comes from rocks. Rocks have salt in them. When rocks are worn down by water, the salt goes into the water.

12"
12" 12"
SALT 1 LB.
SALT 1 LB.
One cubic foot of seawater has over 2 pounds of salt in it.

MOST OF THE SALT IN THE OCEAN IS THE SAME KIND WE PUT ON FOOD.

SALADS   HOT LUNCH

The next day, everyone showed up
in a bathing suit.
We boarded the old school bus,
and Frizzie started the engine.
We were ready for a day of
fun in the sun!

TIDES RISE AND FALL EVERY DAY
by Rachel

When the water near shore rises and gets deep, it is high tide.
When the water falls and gets shallow, it is low tide.

HIGH TIDE   LOW TIDE

Tides are caused mostly by the pull of the moon's gravity on the earth and its oceans.

"We are now in the intertidal zone," said Ms. Frizzle.
"That is the part of shore that is covered with water at high tide, and uncovered at low tide."

HERE I AM SAVING A GRANDMOTHER... AND THIS IS MY FAMOUS RESCUE OF MUFFY, A BELOVED FAMILY PET.

MM-HM

MM-HM

Out the windows we saw tide pools —
puddles of water left on shore
when the tide goes out.
We were hoping the Friz would let us out,
but no such luck.
She kept driving full speed ahead.

WE ARE HERE

TIDE POOL
HIGH TIDE
LOW TIDE
INTERTIDAL ZONE

SS SCHOOL BUS

SHE SAID WE WERE GOING TO THE BEACH.

NO, SHE DIDN'T. SHE SAID WE WERE GOING TO THE OCEAN.

I GUESS SHE REALLY MEANT IT!

Seaweeds

Sea Stars

Periwinkles

Limpets

Mussels

Barnacles

Green Crabs

Sea Urchins

Suddenly a mysterious wave rose up.
Ms. Frizzle opened the door of the bus,
and the lifeguard was swept inside.
Outside the windows
we saw nothing but rushing water.
We screamed and closed our eyes.

HOW CAN FISH BREATHE UNDERWATER?
by Amanda Jane
People have lungs that take oxygen from air.
Fish have gills that can take oxygen from water.

OXYGEN DISSOLVED IN WATER
WATER
WATER
GILLS TAKE IN OXYGEN
WATER PASSES THROUGH

Water flows into the fish's mouth, then the gills, and out through slits in the fish's sides.

Sponges

Ms. Frizzle decided this was a good moment for us to get out of the bus.
Thank goodness we had air tanks!
All around us were fish, fish, and more fish.
"Many kinds of fish swim in large groups called *schools*," said Ms. Frizzle.

LOOK! A SCHOOL OF FISH!

LOOK! A SCHOOL OF CHILDREN!

I WISH WE HAD A BUS.

Down below, on the muddy bottom,
lobsters were catching crabs.
Starfish used their arms
to pry open clamshells.
And jellyfish floated past,
catching small fish
with their stinging tentacles.
The ocean was teeming with life!

Medusa Jellyfish

MOST OF THE SEAFOOD WE EAT COMES FROM HERE ON THE CONTINENTAL SHELF, ARNOLD.

I THOUGHT IT CAME FROM THE SUPERMARKET SHELF.

Blue Crab

Lobster

WHELKS

Sea Star

Clam

Blue Scallops

Q: WHEN IS A FISH NOT A FISH?
A: WHEN IT'S A JELLYFISH!
by Gregory

A true fish has a backbone, gills and fins. Some animals are called "fish" but they are not. Actually, they are _invertebrates_, animals without backbones.

Here are some of them:

Jellyfish

Sea Star
(also called starfish)

shellfish

SCALLOP   MUSSEL   SNAIL   CRAB

SHARKS ARE FISH
by Molly
Most sharks are fast swimmers with razor-sharp teeth. Usually they eat ocean animals like crabs, fish, seals— even other sharks.

SOME KINDS OF SHARKS
GREAT WHITE →
← HAMMERHEAD
THRESHER →
NURSE →

A DIFFERENT KIND OF SKELETON
by Ralph
Sharks do not have bones like other fish. Their skeleton is made of cartilage. This is the same bendable material that is in your ears and the tip of your nose.

Oh, no! The shapes were tiger sharks!
Ms. Frizzle told us not to worry.
She said most sharks will not eat people.
"The number of people killed by sharks every year is very, very small,"
said Ms. Frizzle.
We panicked anyway!

Tiger Sharks

HUMANS ARE NOT THE MAIN DIET OF TIGER SHARKS BUT THEY MAY ATTACK IF HUMANS ARE NEARBY.

UH-OH! WE'RE NEARBY!

Then an enormous whale shark slid by.
"Whale sharks never hurt people.
They eat nothing but plankton,"
said Ms. Frizzle.
The giant shark swam down, and we went along.
We were leaving the continental shelf, following
a steep cliff called the continental slope.
We were on our way to the deep ocean floor.

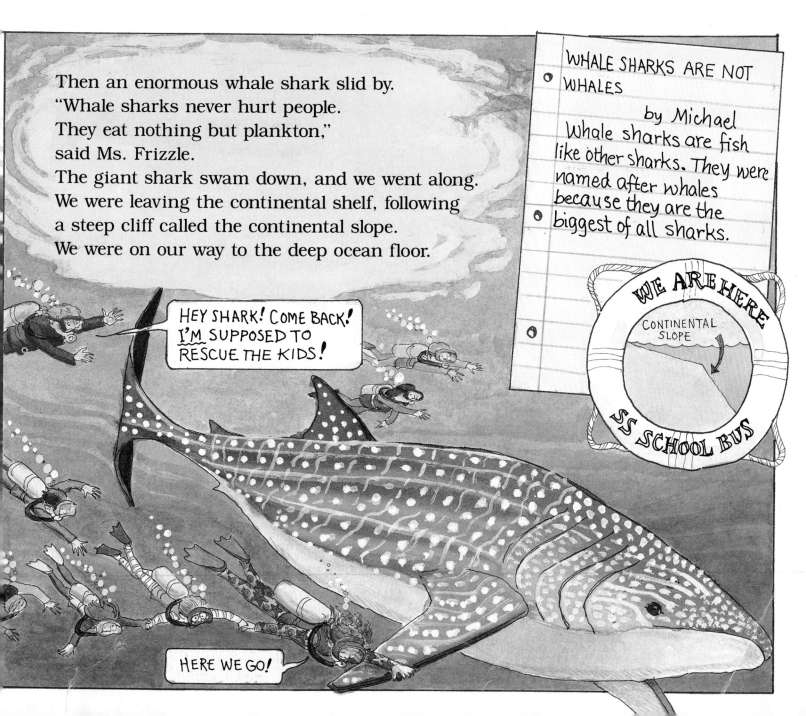

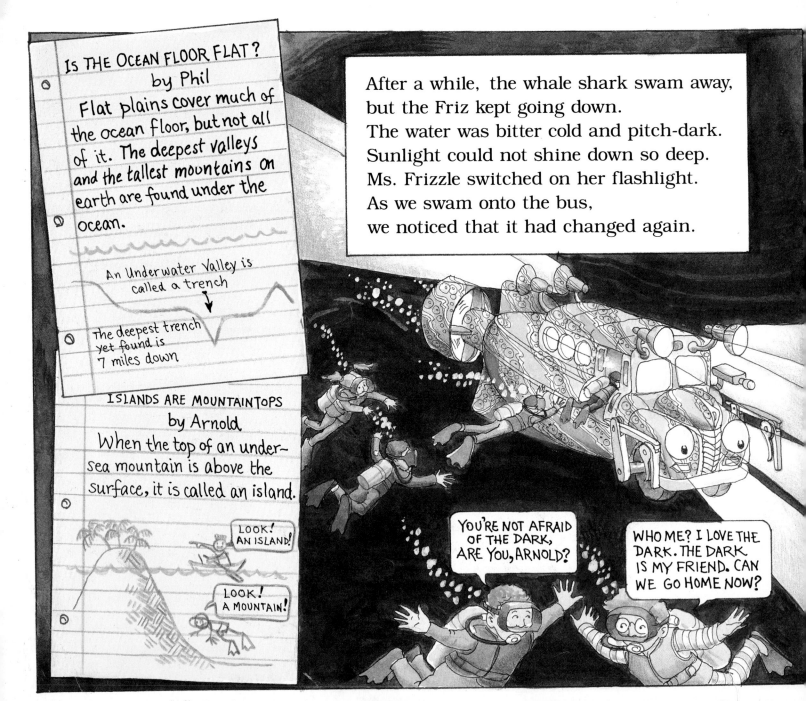

This time it was a *submersible*, a vehicle made for exploring the deep ocean floor. "The pressure down here would crush an ordinary submarine," Frizzie explained, and she drove all the way to the bottom. "There is not enough food here for large animals," Ms. Frizzle told us. "Most deep-sea fish are tiny." The deep ocean floor was as empty as an underwater desert!

THOSE TINY DEEP-SEA FISH CAN GLOW IN THE DARK.

THEY HAVE THEIR OWN SPECIAL LIGHT, JUST AS FIREFLIES DO ON LAND.

SWALLOWER

ANGLER FISH

LANTERN FISH

HATCHET FISH

WE ARE HERE
Shelf
Slope
Deep Ocean Floor
SS SCHOOL BUS

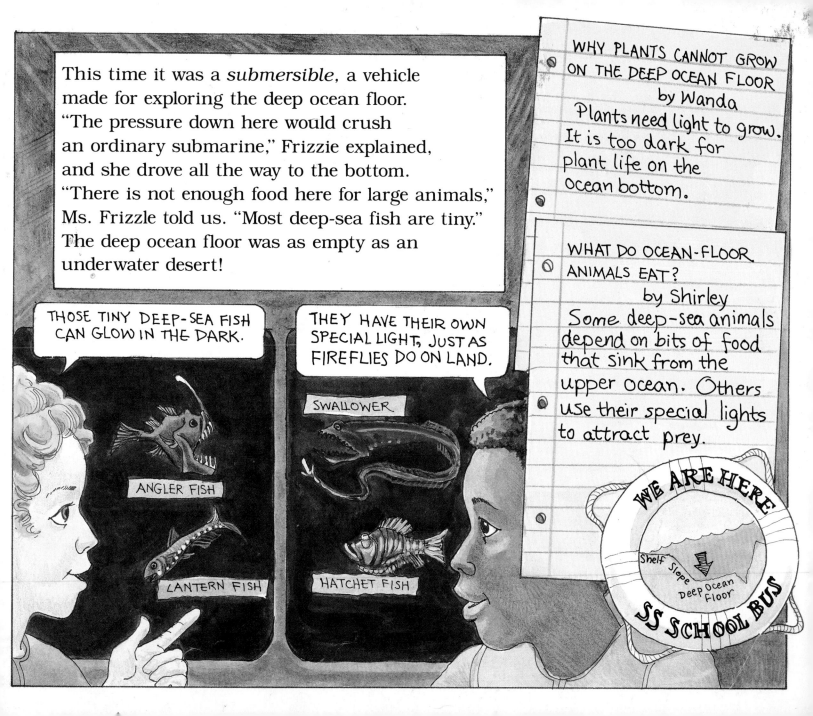

WHAT CAUSES [A VENT]
by Alex
A vent is formed when seawater seeps into cracks in the ocean floor. The water touches super-hot rocks inside the earth. Then the hot water shoots up out of the vent.

WATER

LAVA

HOW FOOD IS MADE AT A VENT
by Shirley
Special bacteria manufacture their own food using heat energy and hydrogen sulfide gas from the vent. This food supports much of the life at the vent.

Then up ahead, we saw a spot that was full of life. It looked like an undersea garden with all kinds of strange animals in it.

"This is a hot-water *vent*, class," said the Friz. "A vent is an opening in the ocean floor. Flowing from the vent is super-hot water mixed with hydrogen sulfide gas."

AT A HOT-WATER VENT THERE IS ENOUGH FOOD FOR MANY LARGE ANIMALS.

THESE TUBE WORMS LOOK LIKE HUGE LIPSTICKS

HUGE CLAMS (1 FOOT OR MORE)

GIANT TUBE WORMS (8 TO 10 FEET)

HOW IS A CORAL REEF BUILT?
by Amanda Jane

Each coral polyp grows a stony skeleton around itself. The reef is made of a layer of living coral animals attached to a wall of many millions of dead skeletons.

Actual sizes of typical coral polyps

Each "pock mark" is a single coral animal.

HOW CORAL POLYPS EAT
by Rachel

Most corals feed at night. Tiny arms come out of a coral's stony skeleton. The arms catch plankton and pass it into the coral's mouth.

MOUTH
ARMS
SKELETON

CORAL POLYP IN THE DAYTIME

THE SAME POLYP AT NIGHT

Soon we were motoring over the open ocean toward a sun-drenched island.
The bus had changed into a glass-bottom boat.
Through the glass, we saw what looked like a wall made of colorful rocks.
Ms. Frizzle said it was a coral reef, made of tiny animals called coral *polyps*.
We dove overboard and began to explore.

DON'T SWIM FAR! I HAVEN'T FINISHED SAVING YOU YET!

OH, HAS HE STARTED ALREADY?

I'M SURE HE'S DOING HIS BEST.

SEA PENS

The reef was made of many different kinds of corals.
Some looked like trees with branches.
Others looked like fans or fingers.
Some even looked like human brains!

THREE KINDS OF CORAL REEFS
by Tim

1. A fringing reef is attached to the shore.

TOP VIEW SIDE VIEW
← REEF →

2. A barrier reef has a channel of water between it and the shore.
← WATER

3. An atoll is a ring of coral around a sunken volcano.
SUNKEN VOLCANO →

WE ARE HERE
ISLAND
FRINGING REEF

MS. FRIZZLE AND THE KIDS ARE ON A FRINGING REEF ATTACHED TO THE SHORE OF AN ISLAND. BUS

"A coral reef makes a good home
for many ocean plants and animals,"
said the Friz.
We saw crabs and lobsters,
huge eels and octopuses,
slimy sea slugs and spiny sea urchins,
and the most colorful fish in the world.

SMILE, EVERYONE!

I ALWAYS KNEW I WAS A STAR.

MORAY EEL

GIANT CLAM

SEA HARE

Too soon, Ms. Frizzle said it was time to go.
No one wanted to be left behind
so we all climbed aboard.
Frizzie stepped on the gas,
and the bus chugged away from the coral reef.

MAMMALS IN THE SEA
by Florrie

Animals such as dolphins, whales, seals and walruses are not fish. They are warm-blooded mammals like horses, dogs and human beings.

Most fish lay eggs but mammals do not. Mother mammals give birth to live young and feed their babies with milk.

Nearby, a school of dolphins leaped past. In the distance, we saw a whale. Everything seemed normal. Then we noticed that something weird was happening. The bus was getting *flat*.

As usual, Ms. Frizzle was the only one who stayed calm.
She drove us to an ocean current, and we were swept along in the fast-moving water for thousands of miles.
After a while, we saw our beach again.

RIVERS IN THE OCEAN
by Phoebe
Parts of the ocean flow like rivers. These moving areas are called ocean currents.

TELL ME, KIDS, IS YOUR BUS ALWAYS LIKE THIS?

WELL IT'S NEVER BEEN A BOAT BEFORE...

AND IT'S NEVER BEEN FLAT BEFORE...

BUT OTHERWISE IT HASN'T CHANGED.

KEEP YOUR BALANCE, CLASS.

WHY DO BIG WAVES "BREAK" NEAR SHORE?
by Carmen

In shallow water, the ocean bottom drags on the lower part of the wave and slows it down. The upper part keeps going fast, so it falls over, or breaks.

TOP KEEPS GOING FAST

BOTTOM SLOWS DOWN

"Everyone stay on the bus!"
shouted the Friz.
On the bus was right.
It had turned into a giant surfboard!

We had to stand on top of it.
And we were riding a wild wave
straight toward shore!

Our diving suits were gone,
and the bus was its old self again.
There it was, sitting in the parking lot
as if nothing had happened.
We thanked Lenny for everything
and hit the road.

Back in our classroom,
we made a terrific chart of the ocean
for the bulletin board.

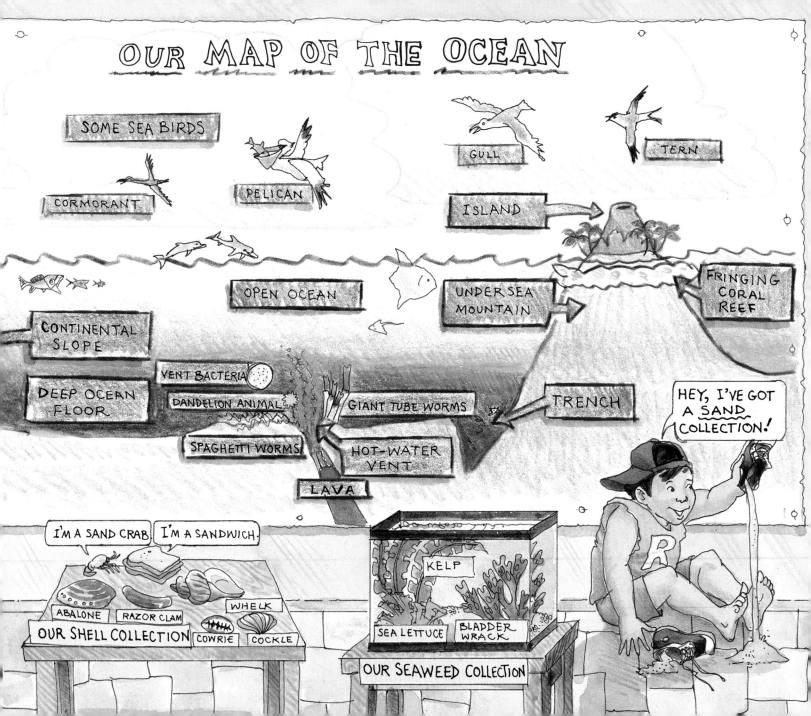

By then we were definitely ready to go home.
Thank goodness it was Friday!
After that class trip
we really *needed* a weekend off!

FIND OUT WHICH THINGS ARE TRUE, AND WHICH THINGS ARE MAKE-BELIEVE!

MULTIPLE-CHOICE TEST

First, read the question. Then read the three answers — A, B, and C. Decide which one is correct. To see if you were right, check the answers on the next page.

QUESTIONS:

1. In real life, what would happen if a school bus drove into the ocean?

   A. The bus would turn into a submarine, then a submersible, then a glass-bottom boat, and finally, a surfboard.

   B. The bus would stay a bus.

   C. The bus would turn into a rubber-ducky.

2. Is it possible to explore the ocean in a single day?

   A. Yes, if you travel by giant clam.

   B. No, you couldn't do it in a day. It would take months, no matter how you made the trip.

   C. Maybe. It depends on how long the day is.

3. In real life, can ocean animals speak?

   A. Yes, but only when they have something important to say.

   B. Yes, but too many bubbles come out.

   C. No. Ocean animals do not talk.

ANSWERS:

1. The correct answer is B. A bus cannot magically change into anything else. It also cannot run under the ocean. Water would seep inside and the bus would sink.

2. The correct answer is B. It takes a long time to travel thousands of miles through water. Even whales need months to migrate from one part of the ocean to another.

3. The correct answer is C. It is true that many fish make sounds, and whales and dolphins seem to communicate in a special way. But ocean animals do not use human language, and no one has ever heard a sea star tell a joke.

Joanna Cole never explored the deep ocean floor in a school bus, but she did spend many summer days at the beach. Growing up near the New Jersey shore, Ms. Cole's fondest memories of the ocean include collecting shells and crabs, building sand castles, and riding big ocean waves. Today, Ms. Cole enjoys writing science books for children, including *The Magic School Bus* series. She is the winner of the 1991 *Washington Post*/Children's Book Guild Nonfiction Award for the body of her work. A former teacher and children's book editor, Ms. Cole now writes full time and makes her home in Connecticut with her husband and daughter.

Bruce Degen remembers playing at the Coney Island beach as a youngster. When it was time to get out of the ocean, he always pretended he couldn't hear his mother calling him. In recent years, Mr. Degen has visited other beaches and aquariums to see firsthand some of the fish in this book. He befriended an elephant seal on the shores of California, and is the proud owner of two Humuhumunukunukuapuaa T-shirts. The illustrator of more than two dozen books for children, Mr. Degen lives in Connecticut with his wife and two sons.